THE SCIENCE BEHIND

Communication

Casey Rand

Raintree

www.raintreepublishers.co.uk
Visit our website to find out
more information about
Raintree books.

To order:
☎ Phone 0845 6044371
🖹 Fax +44 (0) 1865 312263
🖳 Email myorders@raintreepublishers.co.uk

Customers from outside the UK please telephone +44 1865 312262

Raintree is an imprint of Capstone Global Library
Limited, a company incorporated in England and
Wales having its registered office at 7 Pilgrim
Street, London, EC4V 6LB – Registered company
number: 6695582

Edited by Megan Cotugno and Laura Knowles
Designed by Richard Parker
Picture research by Mica Brancic
Original Illustrations © Capstone Global Library
   Ltd 2012
Illustrations by Oxford Designers & Illustrators
Originated by Capstone Global Library Ltd
Printed and bound in China by Leo Paper
   Products Ltd

ISBN 978 1 406 23398 8 (hardback)
15 14 13 12 11
10 9 8 7 6 5 4 3 2 1

ISBN 978 1 406 23404 6 (paperback)
17 16 15 14 13
10 9 8 7 6 5 4 3 2 1

British Library Cataloguing in Publication Data
Rand, Casey.
The science behind communication.
302.2-dc22
A full catalogue record for this book is available
from the British Library.

Acknowledgements
We would like to thank the following for
permission to reproduce photographs: Corbis
pp. **10** (Lebrecht Music & Arts/© Lebrecht Authors),
11 (© Bettmann), **17** (ClassicStock/© Camerique),
19 (© Atlantide Phototravel/Stefano Amantini);
ESA p. **21**; Shutterstock pp. **5** (© Oliveromg),
7 (© Pablo77), **8** (© Trombax), **9** (© Patricia
Hofmeester), **12** (© Jhaz Photography), **14**
(© Ericlefrancais), **25** (© Monkey Business Images).

Cover Image of a communications satellite in
space reproduced with permission of ESA.

We would like to thank David Crowther and Nancy
Harris for their invaluable help in the preparation
of this book.

Every effort has been made to contact copyright
holders of any material reproduced in this book.
Any omissions will be rectified in subsequent
printings if notice is given to the publisher.

Contents

Communication 4

Language 6

Long distance 8

Extra! Extra! Read all about it! 10

Communication: it's electric! 12

Television time 16

Wireless revolution 18

The internet 22

Masters of communication 24

Try it yourself 26

Glossary 28

Find out more 30

Index 32

Look for these boxes:

Stay safe
These boxes tell you how to keep yourself and your friends safe from harm.

In your day
These boxes show you how science is a part of your daily life.

Measure up!
These boxes give you some fun facts and figures to think about.

Some words appear in bold, **like this**. You can find out what they mean by looking at the green bar at the bottom of the page or in the glossary.

Communication

Ring, ring! A **telephone** call can be exciting. Imagine a world without phones. Hundreds of years ago, if you wanted to talk to someone in a faraway place, you might have had to pack your bags and travel to them. Before planes, trains, and cars this could take months, or even years!

What is communication?

Communication can be a wink, a thumbs-up, a wave, and a smile. A phone call, email, or text message is communication, too. There are many forms of communication. Any way in which thoughts, ideas, messages, or information is shared is communication.

Did humans invent communication?

New inventions have changed the way in which we **communicate**. However, humans did not invent communication. Animals have been communicating with sounds, smells, colour, and movement since long before humans were around.

telephone   device that changes sound into signals and sends it to distant places, and then changes signals back into sound

Telephones make talking to friends in faraway places fast and easy.

communication	exchange of messages, thoughts, ideas, and information
communicate	exchange messages, thoughts, ideas, and information

Language

The letters on this page are **symbols**. Symbols have special meaning. When you read these letters out loud, the sounds you make have special meaning, too. These sounds and symbols are **language**.

Life without language

Language makes **communicating** with others easier. Imagine being in a faraway place where everyone speaks a different language from you. Asking for directions to the shops would be very difficult! Language allows us to share ideas and information with those around us.

In your day

Learning to read and write takes lots of practice. However, it is easier today than it was thousands of years ago. In English, you have to memorize 26 letters. These form every word. Before the alphabet, a symbol was memorized for each word. So hundreds or thousands of symbols would need to be memorized.

symbol   something which represents something else, such as letters

Many animals have their own languages. Birds sing, dogs bark, and lions roar.

language set of sounds and symbols and the rules for how to use them for communication

Long distance

Sending a letter to a friend today is easy. You can post a written message across the country, or even across the world, in just a few days. Sending mail across the world has not always been so easy.

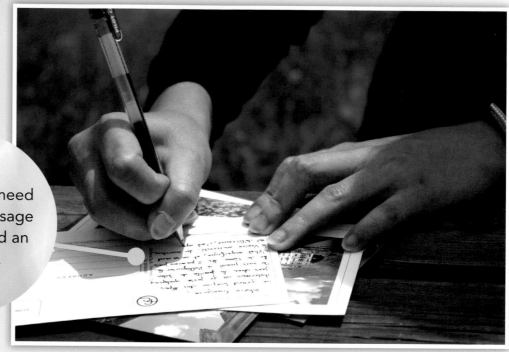

Today all you need to send a message is a stamp and an envelope.

Marathon messengers

For thousands of years, **messengers** carried news and **communication** on foot. The most famous messenger was named Pheidippides. He ran 40 kilometres (25 miles) to deliver news of the Greek victory at the battle of **Marathon**! Today, there is a long running race called a marathon, in memory of the messenger's amazing effort.

messenger   anyone who delivers a message
marathon   long running race named after an ancient Greek village

Pony Express

Before planes, trains, and cars, many important messages were delivered on horseback. During the 1800s a mail service called the Pony Express was formed in the United States. Pony Express stations were about 16 kilometres (10 miles) apart across the western United States. Messages were carried by riders on horseback, who would change to a fresh horse at every station.

This postage stamp was made in memory of the famous Pony Express.

ST. JOSEPH

SACRAMENTO

1860·1960 PONY EXPRESS

UNITED STATES POSTAGE

4c

Extra! Extra! Read all about it!

Hundreds of years ago all books were written by hand! Copying a book by hand takes a very long time. Because of this, books were very expensive. Most people could not afford to buy their own books. Since very few people had their own books, not many people at this time ever learned to read.

Printing machines

The **printing press** is a giant machine which makes **print**. Print is markings or letters made on paper, like the letters in this book. One of the first printing presses was invented in the country of Germany in the mid-1400s.

The printing press made books and newspapers widely available for the first time.

printing press   machine that allows fast printing of books and newspapers
print   marking or letters made on paper

Newspaper

The printing press made it possible to print newspapers. The first newspapers were printed in the 1600s. There was no radio, **television**, or **internet** at that time. Newspapers quickly became the best place to find news and information.

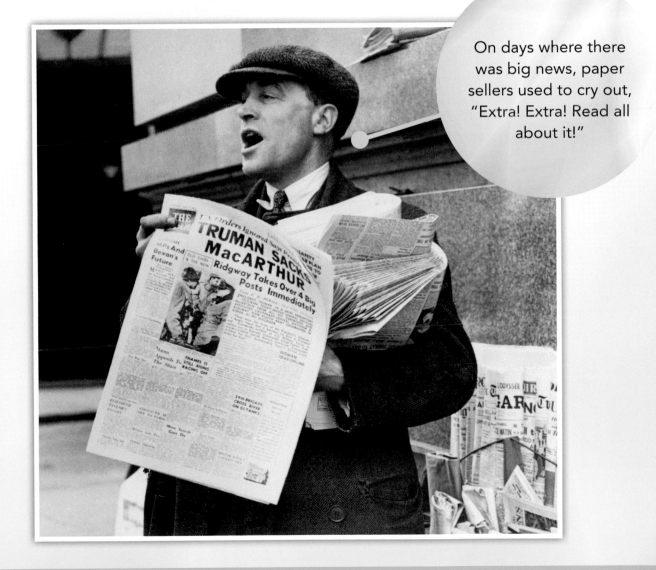

On days where there was big news, paper sellers used to cry out, "Extra! Extra! Read all about it!"

television device that converts signals into moving pictures and sounds
internet system that connects millions of computers around the world

Communication: it's electric!

Communicating with anyone who lived far away used to be very slow. Then, bingo! Humans learned how to use **electricity**.

Electricity

Electricity is a carrier of energy. A flash of lightning during a storm is electricity. This flash may seem to only last a second, but a lightning bolt can travel more than eight kilometres (five miles) during this flash. Electricity travels very fast.

Lightning is a flash of electricity that moves quickly across the sky. Electricity can be used to carry messages from one place to another very quickly.

electricity   form of energy on which information and communication can be sent extremely fast, through wires

Beep, beep! It's the telegraph

The **telegraph** was invented by US inventor Samuel Morse in 1837. This machine allowed pulses (beats) of electricity to be sent along a wire. These pulses were a series of short and long beeps. The beeps made up a special alphabet called **Morse code**. Messages could be sent very quickly using Morse code and electricity.

Person taps out Morse code by pushing down on the button for a short or long time

The button of a telegraph machine was pushed to make short and longer beeps. These beeps raced through a wire, using electricity, to the place the message needed to be sent.

Wire connects to a machine where the Morse code is turned back into letters

When the button is pressed down, an electric pulse is sent along a wire

telegraph   device that sends and receives electric pulses, usually in Morse code, to allow communication

Morse code   code of short and long beeps used to send messages via telegraph

Ring, ring! It's the telephone

A ringing **telephone** can be very exciting. Who could be calling? A friend, a family member, or one of your teachers?

Talk to me

While sending messages in Morse code was fast, people wanted to hear each other's voices. In the 1870s Scottish inventor Alexander Graham Bell found a way to use a telegraph line to send the sound of his voice. Soon everyone would be using telephones.

Telegraphs and telephone calls travelled on electrical wires. By the late 1800s these wires connected major cities around the world.

Going global

Telegraphs and telephone calls had to travel along an electrical wire. So how could a message travel all the way from the United Kingdom to the United States across the Atlantic Ocean? An electric wire had to be laid all the way across the ocean floor! This wire allowed the first telegraphs and phone calls to be sent across the oceans.

Measure up!

Morse code is a **language** made up of short and long beeps. On paper, the short beeps are shown as dots, and the long beeps are shown as dashes. Here is the Morse code alphabet:

A ·—	B —···	C —·—·
D —··	E ·	F ··—·
G ——·	H ····	I ··
J ·———	K —·—	L ·—··
M ——	N —·	O ———
P ·——·	Q ——·—	R ·—·
S ···	T —	U ··—
V ···—	W ·——	X —··—
Y —·——	Z ——··	

Can you work out what this Morse code message says?

·—· · ·— —·· ·· —· ——·

·· ···

··—· ··— —·

Television time

Watching **television** can be very exciting. There are speeding cars, racing trains, distant places, and fairy tales. Television is amazing. But what is even more amazing is the science behind televisions. A film camera on the other side of the world can capture sounds and pictures of what is happening at that moment. These sounds and pictures can travel almost instantly to your television!

Picture this

When you have your school photograph taken, this is a **still picture**. Still pictures are images that do not move. Many magazines, newspapers, and books are filled with still pictures.

In your day

What do still pictures have to do with television? When you watch television it looks like a moving picture. In fact television is just many still pictures taken one after another. Still pictures are flashed on the screen of your television so quickly that they blend together to look like a moving picture.

still picture   image or picture that does not move

Televisions have been around since the 1920s. They have changed a lot since then!

Wireless revolution

These days we can talk on **telephones** in the park, listen to radio in the car, and check email from a train. We do not need wires to **communicate**. **Communication** has gone **wireless**.

Radio waves

Radio waves, like **electricity**, are a form of energy. They can carry messages and information. But radio waves do not travel on a wire. They travel through air. They are invisible and silent, but they are all around us.

radio waves

Radio waves carry music to your radio, films to your **television**, calls to your mobile phone, and much more.

wireless   signals that can be sent without the use of cords, cables, or wires – usually using radio waves

Calling all readers

For almost 100 years after phones were invented they had to be connected to a wire. People could not take their phones with them. The **mobile phones** of today use radio waves. Now phones can go almost anywhere.

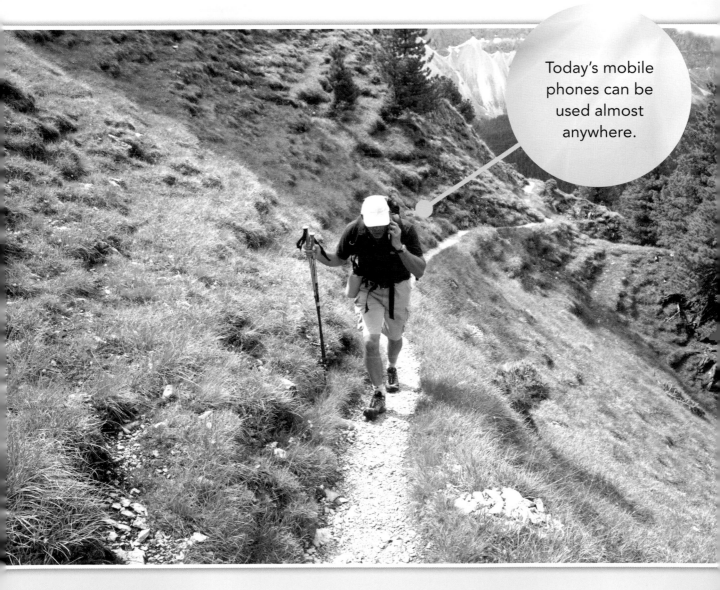

Today's mobile phones can be used almost anywhere.

radio wave type of energy that carries information through the air
mobile phone phone that sends wireless signals by radio waves

Space satellites

If you look up at the night sky you might see a tiny, fast-moving light. You may think this is a shooting star or falling comet, but it is probably a **communication satellite**. These are devices made for communication that fly high above Earth. The satellites send and receive information all around the world.

radio waves

Radio waves are sent from towers on the ground to satellites in the air. The satellites can then send radio waves carrying music, phone calls, and television to your home, school, or car.

communication satellite   device that flies high above the Earth and sends and receives communication to and from Earth

Gravity keeps satellites like this one flying around and around Earth.

Flying around the Earth

Have you ever wondered why the Moon moves around the Earth? The answer is **gravity**. Gravity is what pulls you back to Earth when you jump. It also keeps the Moon flying around the Earth. The pull of gravity keeps communication satellites from flying off into outer space.

gravity   the natural force that pulls you back to Earth when you jump

The internet

Have you used a computer to order pizza, or to find out information about elephants? When you use a computer to do these things you are using the **internet**. The internet connects millions of computers around the world so they can share information. It lets us **communicate** with friends and family, and find out information about almost anything!

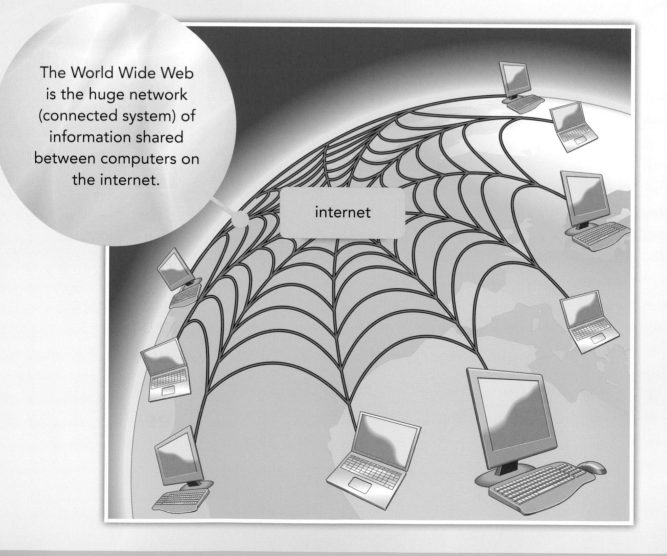

The World Wide Web is the huge network (connected system) of information shared between computers on the internet.

internet

Surfing the web

When you use the internet to search for "elephants", a page will open with information all about elephants. This page is called a **web page**. There are billions of web pages on the internet. They each contain different information. The **World Wide Web** is all of the web pages of information on the internet.

> ## Stay safe
>
> The Internet can be dangerous. Remember these tips:
>
> - Never give out personal information, such as where you live, to anyone on the internet.
>
> - Tell an adult if anything you see on the internet makes you feel uncomfortable.
>
> - Never post or send pictures of yourself on the internet without a parent or guardian's permission.

web page   any of the pages that make up the World Wide Web
World Wide Web   all of the pages of information on the Internet

Masters of communication

While many animals can **communicate**, humans have the most developed **language** system. Language and the alphabet are the most important **communication** technologies of all. Language allows humans to work together.

Print it

The invention of the **printing press** allowed people everywhere to be educated. Before the printing press books were very expensive and very rare. Without many available books, most people never learned to read.

Electricity

The discovery of **electricity** allowed human beings to develop **telegraphs**, **telephones**, radios, **televisions**, and computers. Electricity allowed information to travel around the world very quickly.

No strings attached

Radio waves carry information from one place to another without wires. Radio waves can carry television sound and images from a tower on the ground to a **communication satellite** in space and back to your school in just a few seconds.

The abilities to read, write, speak, listen, see, feel, and smell are the most amazing communication technologies of all.

Try it yourself

Build your own phone

A **telephone** can change sound into a signal. The signal travels on a wire, and is changed back into sound by another phone. You can easily build your own phone to do this. Ask an adult for help before starting.

What you need

- 2 paper cups
- string
- a sharpened pencil

What to do

1. With the sharp pencil, poke a *small* hole through the centre of the bottom of each cup.
2. Cut a piece of string as long as you like, up to about 2 metres (6 ½ feet) long.
3. Poke one end of the string through one of the paper cups and tie a knot inside the cup.
4. Repeat step 3 with the other end of the string and the other cup.

Ready, steady, talk!

Do you think this phone is going to work? Will it work better with the string pulled tightly or loosely? Talk into one cup and ask a friend to see if the sound comes out through the other cup. Try it once with the string tight, and once with the string loose. Which way worked better?

voice vibrates the string

vibrations travel down the string

vibrations turn back into sound

How did it work?

Your voice vibrates (shakes) the string. These vibrations travel down the string. When they reach the other end, they vibrate the bottom of the other cup and turn back into sound.

Glossary

communicate exchange messages, thoughts, ideas, and information

communication exchange of messages, thoughts, ideas, and information

communication satellite device that flies high above Earth and sends and receives communication to and from Earth

electricity form of energy on which information and communication can be sent extremely fast, through wires

gravity the natural force that pulls you back to Earth when you jump

internet system that connects millions of computers around the world so they can share information

language set of sounds and symbols and the rules for how to use them for communication

marathon long running race named after an ancient Greek village

messenger anyone who delivers a message

mobile phone phone that sends wireless signals via radio waves

Morse code code of short and long beeps used to send messages via telegraph

print marking or letters made on paper

printing press machine that allows fast printing of books and newspapers

radio wave type of energy that carries information through the air

still picture image or picture that does not move

symbol something which represents something else, such as letters

telegraph device that sends and receives electric impulses, usually in Morse code, to allow communication

telephone device that changes sound into signals and sends it to distant places, and then changes signals back into sound

television device that converts signals into moving pictures and sounds

web page any of the pages that make up the World Wide Web

wireless signals that can be sent without the use of cords, cables, or wires – usually using radio waves

World Wide Web all of the pages of information on the internet

Find out more

Use these resources to find more fun and useful information about the science behind communication technologies.

Books

Communication (Inventions in...), Ian Graham (QEB Publications, 2008)

The History of the Computer (Inventions That Changed the World), Elizabeth Raum (Heinemann Library, 2008)

The History of the Telephone (Inventions That Changed the World), Elizabeth Raum (Heinemann Library, 2008)

The Printing Press (Tales of Invention), Richard and Louise Spilsbury (Raintree, 2011)

Samuel Morse and the Telegraph (Inventions and Discoveries), David Seidman (Capstone, 2008)

Websites

communication.howstuffworks.com/telephone1.htm
Visit this web page to learn more about how telephones work.

kids.msfc.nasa.gov
This is an interactive and interesting science site for young people.

www.classbraingames.com/2009/12/learn-morse-code
This is a great website that teaches you how to use Morse code. It also has games and activities.

www.bbc.co.uk/schoolradio/subjects/history/victorians/inventions/telephone
Listen to an audio clip about Alexander Graham Bell and the invention of the telephone on this webpage.

Index

alphabets 6, 13, 15, 24
animal communication 4, 7

Bell, Alexander Graham 14
books 10, 16, 24

communication: what it is 4
communication satellites 20, 21, 24
computers 22, 24

electrical wires 13, 14, 15
electricity 12–13, 24
emails 4, 18
energy 12, 18

gravity 21

ideas, sharing 4, 6
Internet 11, 22–23

languages 6, 15, 24
letters 8
lightning 12

marathon 8, 9
messages 4, 8, 9, 12, 13, 14, 15
messengers 8
mobile phones 18, 19
Moon 21
Morse, Samuel 13
Morse code 13, 14, 15

networks 22
newspapers 11, 16

Pheidippides 8
Pony Express 9
print 10
printing presses 10–11, 24

radio waves 18, 19, 20, 24
reading and writing 6, 10, 24

safety 23
satellites 20, 21, 24
still pictures 16
symbols 6

telegraphs 13, 14, 15, 24
telephones 4, 5, 14–15, 18, 19, 24, 26–27
television 11, 16–17, 18, 24
text messages 4

vibrations 27

web pages 23
wireless communication 18–19
World Wide Web 22, 23